An Encycl
ROCKS

Ken Greene

Contents

Rigby®

A Harcourt Achieve Imprint

www.Rigby.com
1-800-531-5015

Rocks and More Rocks

Everywhere you look you can see rocks. Mountains and canyons are rocks. There are rocks in the soil and rocks on the beach. Even some buildings are made from rocks. Rocks can be small like pebbles, flat like skipping stones, or big like boulders. There are many kinds of rocks, but what is a rock?

A rock is made of one or more **minerals**. There are more than 4,000 different kinds of minerals, but only about 100 are common enough to be found in a variety of places. Even if a mineral is found in many different places, it always looks the same.

Quartz, mica, olivine, and feldspar are four of the most common rock-forming minerals.

quartz

mica

olivine

feldspar

Geologists collect small pieces of rock so they can study the rock closely. They try to find out what the rock is made of and when it was formed.

The study of rocks is called **geology**, and the people who study rocks are called geologists. Geologists study rocks on mountains, in caves, underwater, and even around live volcanoes! They look at how rocks have changed and continue to change over time.

The Three Types of Rocks

Although minerals always look the same, the same kind of rock can look different from place to place. This happens when the minerals that make up the rock appear in different amounts. It can also happen when the minerals combine under different temperatures.

Because the same kind of rock can look different in different locations, geologists have to play detective to find out what a rock is made up of and how it was formed. Once they figure this out, they place the rock into one of three groups.

Geologists have to act like detectives to solve the mysteries of some rocks!

Sedimentary Rocks

sandstone

Sedimentary rocks are made from many layers of **sediment**, such as soil, sand, clay, and sometimes plants and animals that have died. As sediment piles up over time, pressure builds on the bottom layers. The different layers of sediment are squeezed together tightly. After millions and millions of years, these layers, called **strata**, become cemented together to form sedimentary rock, such as sandstone.

Igneous Rocks

basalt

Igneous rocks are made from hot, liquid rock called **magma**, which is found deep inside the earth. As magma rises toward the earth's surface, it starts to cool. Depending on how slow or fast the magma cools, different kinds of igneous rocks, such as basalt, are formed.

Metamorphic Rocks

marble

Metamorphic rocks form thousands of feet under the earth's surface. The heat and pressure deep inside the earth change the old rock into new kinds of rock, such as marble.

The Rock Cycle

Rocks are always changing. Water or wind can break down the huge rocks on mountains into pieces. A stream or river can carry the rock pieces, or sediment, for a long way before they settle to the bottom of the river. Layers of sediment build up in the riverbed. After a very long time, new sedimentary rocks form.

Rocks can be changed by four main forces.
- **Weathering**: Wind, sun, and ice can break rocks into smaller pieces.
- **Erosion**: Water and wind can slowly wear away, or erode, rocks and carry the small pieces to a new place.
- **Temperature**: When rocks are heated or cooled, they can change form. Heating usually happens far underground. Cooling usually happens closer to the surface of the earth.
- **Stress**: The force put on a rock by something pushing against it can change a rock.

Most rock changes take millions of years. The materials from which rocks are made can never be destroyed—rocks are just changed from one kind of rock into another. Geologists call the way rocks change the rock cycle.

Rocks can be weathered, eroded, and turned into **sediment**.

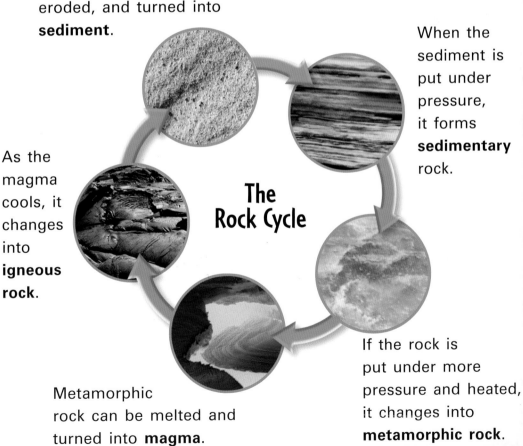

The Rock Cycle

When the sediment is put under pressure, it forms **sedimentary** rock.

As the magma cools, it changes into **igneous rock**.

Metamorphic rock can be melted and turned into **magma**.

If the rock is put under more pressure and heated, it changes into **metamorphic rock**.

Amphibolite

amphibolite

Amphibolite is a dark green or black metamorphic rock. Sometimes white spots in the rock give it a "salt-and-pepper" look. It has a rough **texture**, and it is heavy. Amphibolite is used to build roads because of its strength and ability to last a long time.

Did You Know?

Amphibolite got its name from the Greek word *amphibolos,* which means "having more than one meaning." The minerals in amphibolite are easily mistaken for other minerals.

Amphibolite is made when certain igneous or sedimentary rocks are heated and put under pressure. Amphibolite is found in mountain regions in the United States, France, England, Germany, and Scandinavia. It is usually mixed in with other kinds of rock. Layers of amphibolite make zigzag patterns in the sides of mountains.

Amphibolite is crushed and added to other road building materials to make them stronger.

Basalt

basalt

Basalt is the most common rock on the surface of the earth. Basalt is gray or black, and it can feel rough or smooth when touched. Basalt is made from magma, which rises from under the ground and breaks through cracks and volcanoes on the earth's surface. When the hot lava flow cools, it can turn into basalt rock.

Did You Know?

The Rosetta Stone, which is made of basalt, has writing carved on it in Egyptian hieroglyphs (picture writing) and Greek. This stone helped scientists learn how to read Egyptian hieroglyphs.

Even though much of the earth is covered in basalt, it is not usually seen because most basalt is found on the ocean floor. Basalt can be seen on islands, such as the Hawaiian Islands, that were made from volcanoes erupting under the ocean or on coastlines. Basalt has also been found on the moon, and it is thought that basalt forms the volcanoes on Mars and Venus, too.

The Giant's Causeway in Northern Ireland is made of columns of basalt.

Coal

coal

Coal is a black, shiny, sedimentary rock. It is different from other rocks because it is made from plants. A long time ago when the earth was partly covered by swampy forests, plants grew, died, and sank to the bottom of the swamps. The dead plants were covered with layers of water and dirt. Over millions of years, heat and pressure from the top layers turned the dead plants into coal.

How Coal Was Formed

Plants that existed hundreds of millions of years ago died in swamps.

Water and dirt buried the plants far beneath the earth's surface.

Heat and pressure from the layers above turned the dead plants into coal.

12

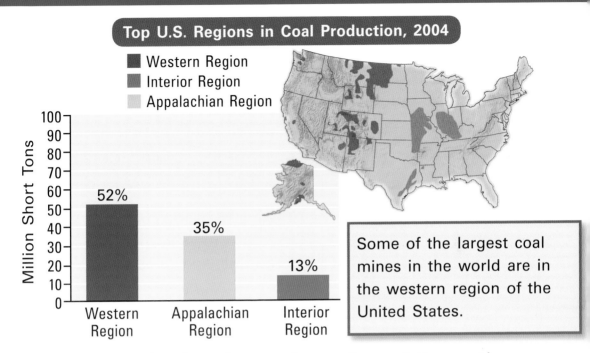

Top U.S. Regions in Coal Production, 2004

- Western Region
- Interior Region
- Appalachian Region

Million Short Tons

52%	35%	13%
Western Region	Appalachian Region	Interior Region

Some of the largest coal mines in the world are in the western region of the United States.

Coal can be found near the surface of the earth, sometimes less than 200 feet underground. It can also be found buried from several hundred feet to more than one thousand feet below the surface. Coal miners use huge machines to remove the coal from deep in the ground.

Coal can be burned and used as fuel. In power plants, coal is burned to heat water, which makes steam. This steam is then used to run machines that produce electricity. Coal is also used in the making of steel, plastics, and even some medicines.

Dolerite

dolerite

Dolerite is similar to basalt because it also forms when liquid magma cools. However, the magma cools slower when dolerite is formed, giving dolerite a rougher texture than basalt. Dolerite is very hard and is used in repairing roads and sidewalks.

This dolerite wall, known as the Whin Sill, was formed when magma pushed up through the earth's surface and cooled. It runs over 84 miles from Scotland to England. In some places the wall is more than 200 feet thick!

Did You Know?

Even though dolerite is usually dark gray, brown, or black, it is sometimes called bluestone.

No one knows for sure who built the large stone circle at Stonehenge or why it was built.

Dolerite was used to build Stonehenge in Wiltshire, England. The large stone circle was built between 3000-2000 B.C. It is believed that the dolerite came from the region that is now Wales, but no one knows exactly how the heavy rocks were moved to England.

Dolomite

Dolomite, also called dolostone, is a sedimentary rock made from a single mineral. It is gray to yellowish-gray in color. Dolomite is used in the steel-making process and in making cement.

dolomite

Dolomite is used to make steel.

A large area of dolomite can be found in the Alps in northern Italy, a favorite place for rock climbers. Some of the dolomite rock **formations** are almost one mile high.

A section of the Alps is called the Dolomites, after the rock the mountains are made of. The Dolomites are famous for the beautiful colors the mountains turn at sunrise and sunset.

Granite

hornblende granite

Granite is one of the most common igneous rocks. It is a heavy and strong rock. When it is polished, granite is beautiful and smooth. This rock can be red, pink, gray, white, black, or any combination of these colors.

For hundreds of years, people have used granite to make buildings and monuments. Today, granite is also used to make kitchen countertops.

Did You Know?

The ancient Egyptians used granite to build obelisks, or tall stone columns.

Many mountains, such as the Sierra Nevada in California and the Black Hills of South Dakota, are made of granite. The faces of four U.S. presidents are carved into the side of Mount Rushmore in the Black Hills. Also in the Black Hills is Devils Tower National Monument, a stump-shaped granite formation that challenges many mountain climbers.

Devils Tower National Monument

Mount Rushmore

19

Limestone

limestone

Limestone is a sedimentary rock that can be white, gray, or pink. This rock usually forms in warm shallow seas as the warm water leaves behind layers of sediment containing shells and skeletons of sea animals. This rock is soft and can easily crumble or crack. Structures made from limestone can wear down very quickly.

Limestone often contains many fossils from sea animals.

aqueduct

There are many uses for limestone. It is used in the making of cement and some kinds of building stone. Farmers even mix it in with the soil to make their crops grow better. Believe it or not, limestone is also ground up and used to make glass!

Did You Know?

The Canadian Rockies are made of a type of limestone. The limestone in the steep cliffs is between 135 and 350 million years old.

Marble

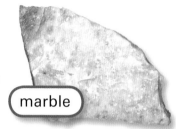

marble

Marble is metamorphic rock made from limestone or dolomite. When these rocks are put under great heat and pressure, they turn into marble.

If the marble is pure, it is all white. If the marble mixes with different minerals when it is formed, however, it can be many other colors, such as light pink, green, and gray.

Did You Know?

Marble is dull and rough when it is mined out of the ground. It needs to be polished smooth to shine.

polished marble

Because of its strength and beauty, marble has been used in art and buildings for thousands of years. Many monuments throughout the world are made out of marble. Marble is also used for making countertops and fireplaces and for decorating buildings to make them look beautiful.

The Lincoln Memorial in Washington, D.C., and the Taj Mahal in Agra, India, are both made of marble.

Obsidian

Obsidian is lava that cooled very quickly. If the lava had cooled more slowly, it would have turned into granite. But obsidian is very different than granite. It looks like thick, black glass. It also breaks like glass, forming razor sharp edges. For thousand of years, people have used obsidian to make tools for cutting other materials.

obsidian

Most obsidian is dark green, brown, or black.

Many types of obsidian, such as black-and-white snowflake obsidian, are used to make jewelry.

Obsidian can also be used for making jewelry and mirrors. When used for these kinds of objects, the rock is smoothed and polished to shine like glass.

Pumice

pumice

Pumice is an amazing rock because it is the only rock that can float! Pumice is lava that was thrown into the air and cooled. Imagine shaking a can of soda and then opening it up. The bubbly foam that explodes out of the can is like the lava, but instead of getting sticky like soda, the lava hardens and turns into rock.

pumice stones made by a volcano

tourists walk on
a pumice beach

Pumice is lightweight and full of tiny holes. It can be white, tan, or black. It also makes a great scrubbing tool because it can be ground up into a powder and put into polishing creams and cleaning products. It can also be added to concrete and other construction materials to make mixtures lighter.

Quartzite

quartzite

Quartzite is a metamorphic rock formed from sandstone. Buried sandstone is heated and pressed together by the weight of rocks above it. This causes the grains of the mineral quartz in the sandstone to become cemented together and change into quartzite. Some quartzite is over 90 percent quartz.

Quartzite is white, light gray, or yellow to brown in color and sparkles in the sun. It is hard and brittle and breaks easily. Quartzite is often used as a bed for train tracks.

cliffs made of Sioux Quartzite bedrock

Sandstone

sandstone

This sedimentary rock is called sandstone because it is made up of sand grains that are cemented together. Sandstone feels like sandpaper. Its color ranges from cream to red. Sandstone can have striped layers and wavy patterns.

Sandstone is one of the easiest sedimentary rocks to find. Whole deserts can be made of sandstone! Sandstone is also often used to sharpen knives and tools.

The Painted Desert in Arizona looks like the rocks were painted with stripes of red, yellow, blue, and gray. The stripes really come from the many layers of sandstone and other sedimentary rocks that were deposited by water one stripe at a time.

Slate

slate

Slate is formed from sedimentary rocks. A sedimentary rock such as shale becomes buried and is put under pressure. The heat and pressure from the earth change the shale into slate. The new rock is harder and stronger than the shale.

Slate can be dark gray, blue-gray, red, green, brown, or purple. Sometimes it has spots or stripes. Slate is found in mountains such as the Appalachians in New York and the Alps in Europe.

Did You Know?

Slate is not always gray. It can be red, green, or even purple!

slate split into sheets

30

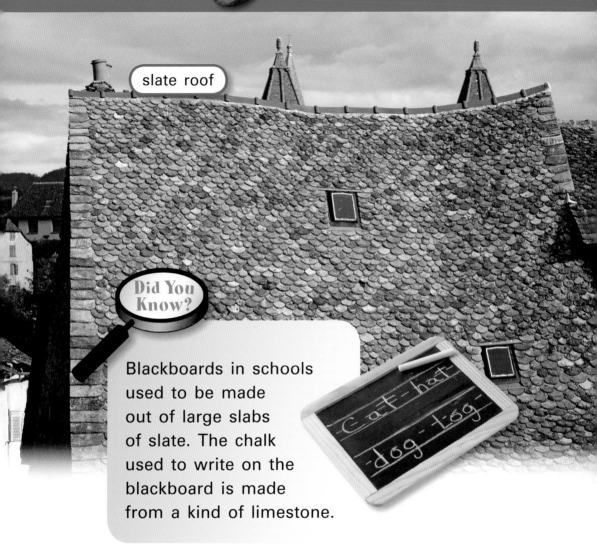

slate roof

Did You Know?

Blackboards in schools used to be made out of large slabs of slate. The chalk used to write on the blackboard is made from a kind of limestone.

Slate can be split into sheets of rock. These thin, strong pieces of slate can be used for many things including roof shingles, tabletops, walkways, and floor tiles.

Glossary

formations rock structures created by forces of nature

geology the study of the history of Earth through its rocks

magma melted rock

minerals non-living, solid matter, usually dug from the ground

sediment small pieces of mud, rock, and soil that have been carried by water or wind and left on the ground

strata layers

texture the feel of something